# Flatpicking Guitar Songs

## Book with Audio Access
## by Bert Casey

All of the songs in this course are played at two speeds on the Audio Tracks. They are available at the following address on the internet:

http://cvls.com/extras/flatpicking/

Copyright 2017 by Watch & Learn, Inc. / Bert Casey 2nd Edition
ALL RIGHTS RESERVED. Any copying, arranging, or adapting of this work without the consent of the owner is an infringement of copyright.

# INTRODUCTION

Flatpicking Guitar Songs is a collection of popular bluegrass guitar solos with very balanced, high quality arrangements. Each song has several variations in order to show what is possible with flatpicking. Many licks and ideas have been intentionally included, which prior to this publication, were passed from guitar player to guitar player at bluegrass festivals.

The Audio Tracks that accompanies this book will enable the student to learn 3 or 4 times faster than with other methods. The Audio Tracks provides the accent, tone, and rhythm for all the songs in this book. Each selection is played slow and fast to make learning much easier.

# THE AUTHOR

Bert Casey, the author of this book has been playing and teaching flatpicking guitar for over 25 years. He has studied and been influenced by the styles of such flatpickers as Doc Watson, Dan Crary, Clarence White, and Tony Rice. Bert plays several instruments (acoustic guitar, electric guitar, bass, mandolin, banjo, ukulele, and flute) and has written 7 other instructional courses *(Acoustic Guitar Primer, Acoustic Guitar Book 2, Electric Guitar Primer, Bass Guitar Primer, Mandolin Primer, Ukulele Primer, and Bluegrass Fakebook)*. He is a professional instructor at ABC Music, which he owns. He also records extensively in his studio, where he has done the sound track to several movies. Bert performed several years with Home Remedy and is currently performing in the Atlanta area with his band Blue Moon.

### *LET US KNOW WHAT YOU THINK*

Hundreds of hours were spent developing this method based on experience with teaching students. Our goal is to provide high quality material at a reasonable price and we constantly improve the product based on your needs. We are concerned that these books are useful and valuable to your progress as a guitarist. Send any comments or suggestions regarding our books and videos to:

Watch & Learn, Inc.
2947 East Point St
East Point, GA 30344
800-416-7088

# AUDIO ACCESS

All of the material in *Flatpicking Guitar Songs* is played on the Audio Tracks at two speeds (slow for practicing and up tempo for performing). These tracks are available at the following address on the internet:

http://cvls.com/extras/flatpicking/

# OTHER BOOKS

If you feel this course is too advanced or you need to brush up on your bluegrass rhythm guitar, try the Acoustic Guitar course.

**Acoustic Guitar Primer Deluxe Edition Book/DVD/2 Jam CDs** by Bert Casey. Designed to take the beginner through the basics of playing bluegrass rhythm guitar. Covers proper hand positions, tuning, scales, rhythm (chords & strumming, bass notes, and bass runs) and lead playing. Utilizes many popular bluegrass standards to play and sing along with. Songs include *Tom Dooley, He's Got The Whole World, Lonesome Road Blues, Worried Man Blues, Roll In My Sweet Baby's Arms, Banks of the Ohio, Dark Hollow, In The Pines, Amazing Grace, Pallet On Your Floor, Way Downtown, Sittin' On Top of the World, Wabash Cannonball, Crying Holy, Salt River, Billy In The Lowground, Little Maggie, Nine Pound Hammer, Wildwood Flower, John Hardy, Old Joe Clark, Blackberry Blossom, & Will The Circle Be Unbroken.*

Book/DVD/2 Jam CDs $19.95

**Bluegrass Fakebook** by Bert Casey. This handy book contains lyrics, chord progressions, and melody lines to 150 of the all-time favorite Bluegrass songs, including 50 gospel tunes as well as many "new" bluegrass songs. Printed in large, easy-to-read type with one song per page, this book is excellent for use on stage or in jam sessions, because everyone can read along. Also includes chord charts for the guitar, banjo, and mandolin and a listing of currently available recordings of each song. Now all those obscure verses you can never remember are right at your fingertips. $19.95

You can find all of these products at your local music store or check our website: http://www.cvls.com. There are also many free lessons for guitar and other instruments on the website.

# TABLE OF CONTENTS

SECTION I - TABLATURE                              Page

- Tablature . . . . . . . . . . . . . . . . . . . . . . . . .2
- Techniques . . . . . . . . . . . . . . . . . . . . . . .3
- Timing . . . . . . . . . . . . . . . . . . . . . . . . . . .5
- Tuning . . . . . . . . . . . . . . . . . . . . . . . . . . .6

SECTION II - THE SONGS

- Will The Circle Be Unbroken . . . . . . . . . . . .8
- Wildwood Flower . . . . . . . . . . . . . . . . . . .9
- Home Sweet Home . . . . . . . . . . . . . . . . .12
- Cripple Creek . . . . . . . . . . . . . . . . . . . . .16
- Red Haired Boy . . . . . . . . . . . . . . . . . . .18
- Nine Pound Hammer . . . . . . . . . . . . . . . .22
- Sally Goodin . . . . . . . . . . . . . . . . . . . . . .26
- Old Joe Clark . . . . . . . . . . . . . . . . . . . . .29
- Black Mountain Rag . . . . . . . . . . . . . . . .33
- Salt River . . . . . . . . . . . . . . . . . . . . . . . .37
- Billy In The Lowground . . . . . . . . . . . . . .41
- John Hardy . . . . . . . . . . . . . . . . . . . . . . .45
- Chord Chart . . . . . . . . . . . . . . . . . . . . . .50

# SECTION 1
# TABLATURE

All of the songs in this course are played at two speeds on the Audio Tracks. They are available at the following address on the internet:

http://cvls.com/extras/flatpicking/

# TABLATURE

This book is written in both tablature and standard music notation. If you wish to learn to read music, consult your local music store for a good book or ask your music teacher for an explanation. We will explain tablature because it is easy to learn if you are teaching yourself and because a lot of popular guitar music is available in tablature.

Tablature is a system for writing music that shows the proper string and fret to play and which fingers to use. It also shows the proper pick direction. In guitar tablature, each line represents a string on the guitar. If the string is to be fretted, the fret number is written on the appropriate line. Otherwise a 0 is written. Study the examples below until you understand them thoroughly.

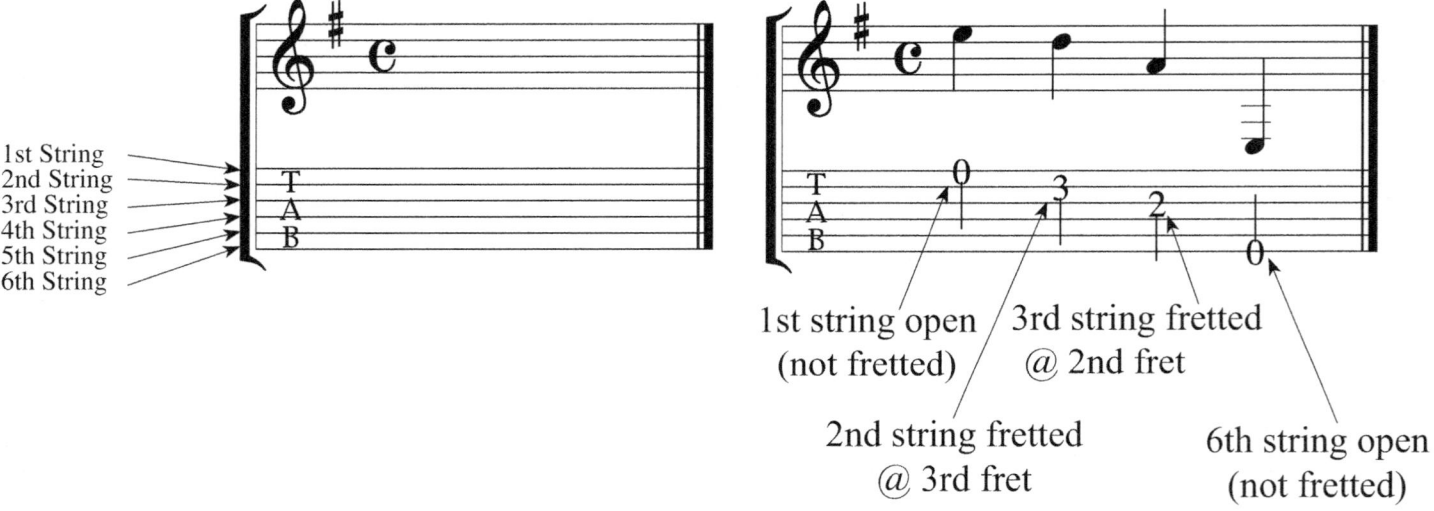

The music will be divided into either two sets of lines (staffs) or three sets of lines.

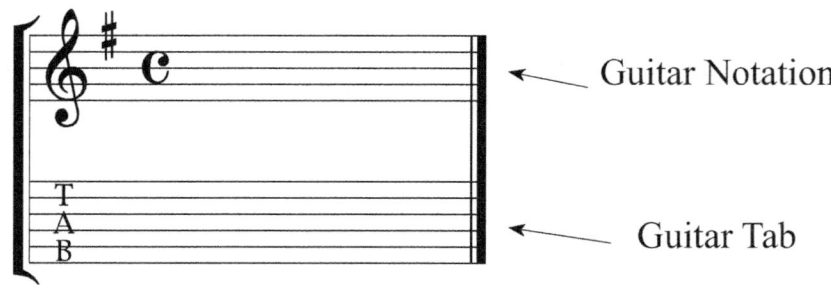

# PICK & STRUM DIRECTION

The correct pick direction is written below the lines and is indicated as follows:

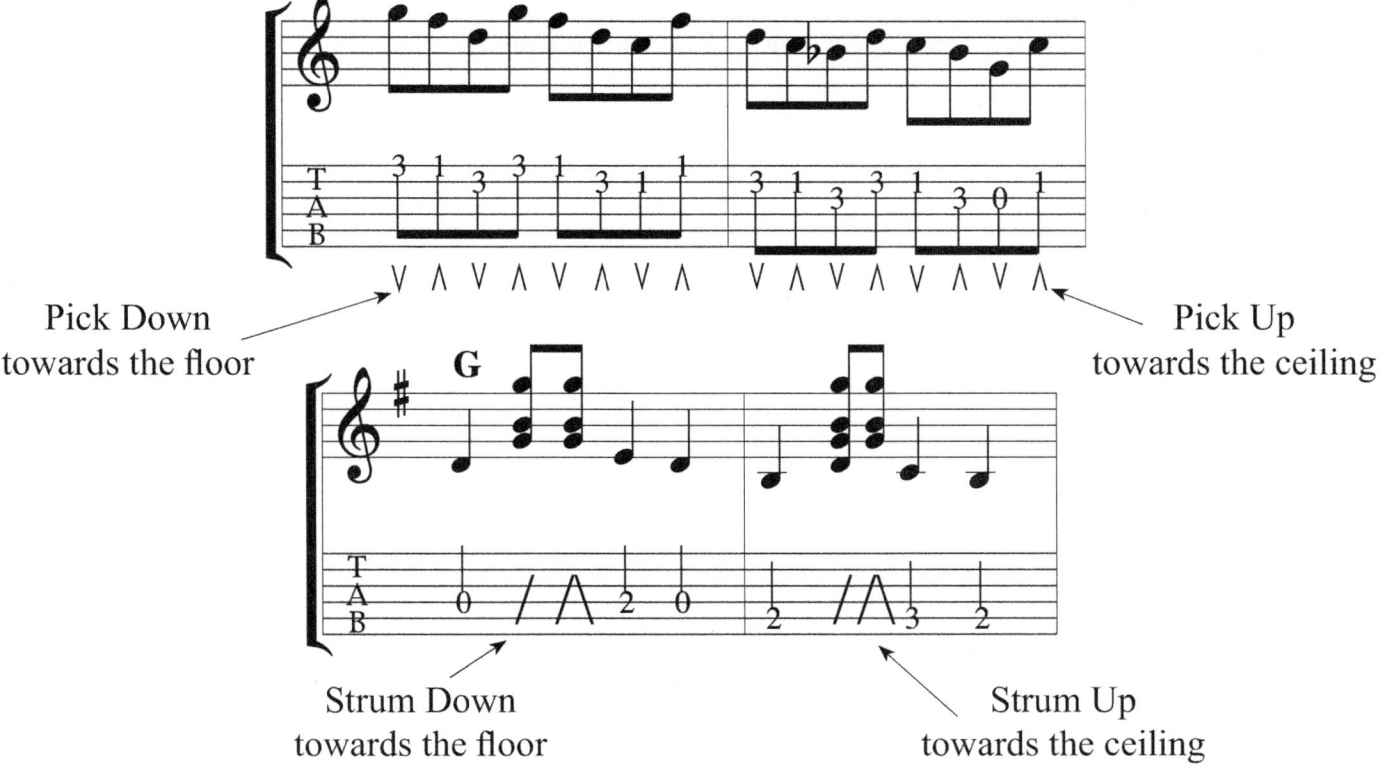

Pick Down towards the floor

Pick Up towards the ceiling

Strum Down towards the floor

Strum Up towards the ceiling

It is extremely important to pay close attention to the pick direction in order to play at the appropriate speed and with the proper timing. It will also enable you to achieve the proper tone.

# LEFT HAND FINGERING

Left hand fingering is written above the tablature.

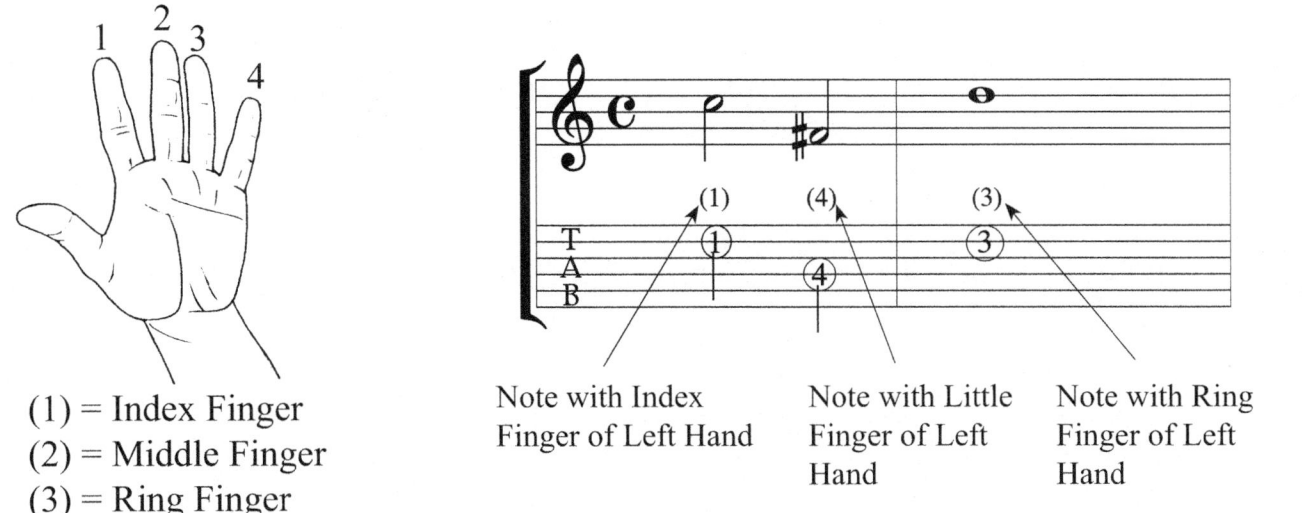

(1) = Index Finger
(2) = Middle Finger
(3) = Ring Finger
(4) = Little Finger

Note with Index Finger of Left Hand

Note with Little Finger of Left Hand

Note with Ring Finger of Left Hand

# REPEAT SIGNS & ENDING

The repeat signs indicate that you are to repeat the section between the two signs. The 1st ending means to repeat back to the beginning of the song, play through the song again, skip the 1st ending and go to the 2nd ending.

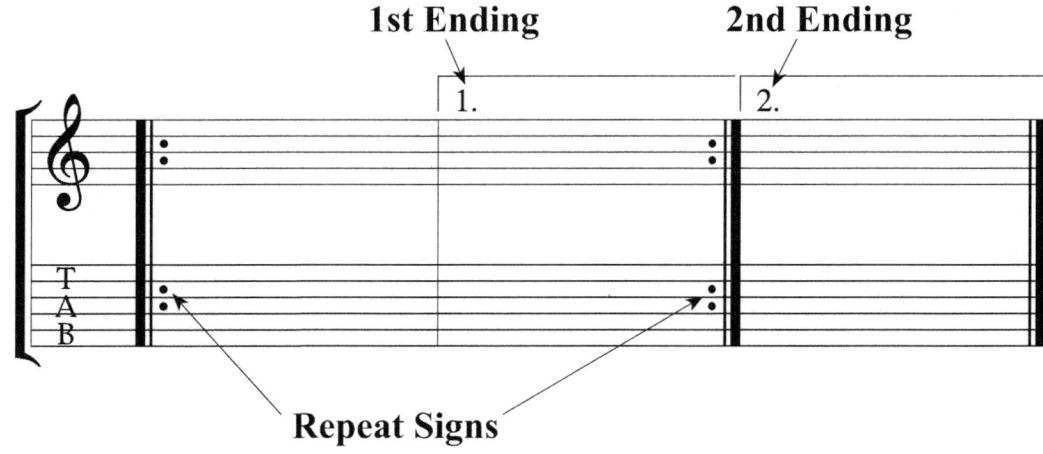

# HAMMER ON, PULL OFF, SLIDE, BEND, STACCATO

Study the following symbols:

| | | |
|---|---|---|
| Hammer on | | From a lower fret to a higher fret. |
| Pull off | | From a higher fret to a lower fret. |
| Slide | | Slide your finger to the appropriate fret. |
| Bend | | Bend the string upwards. |
| Staccato | | Cut the sound off by releasing the pressure with the left hand. |

4

# TIMING

Notes are divided into equal time segments. In this book, there will be 4 beats per measure in each of the songs. In the following example, each line represents 1/2 beat, counted 1 & 2 & 3 & 4 &:

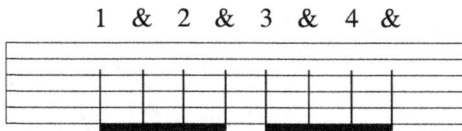

We will use whole notes (4 beats each), half notes (2 beats each), quarter notes (1 beat each), and eighth notes (1/2 beat each) as shown in the following example:

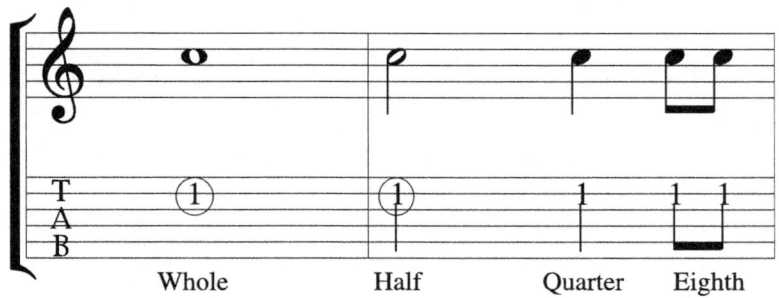

A triplet occurs when 3 notes are played in the space of 2. To count, pronounce triplet as a 3 syllable word (trip-a-let).

If you add the note values of each measure, it will always equal 4 beats.

# TUNING THE GUITAR

Before playing the guitar, it must be tuned to standard pitch. If you have a piano at home, it can be used as a tuning source. The following picture shows which note on the piano to tune each open string of the guitar to.

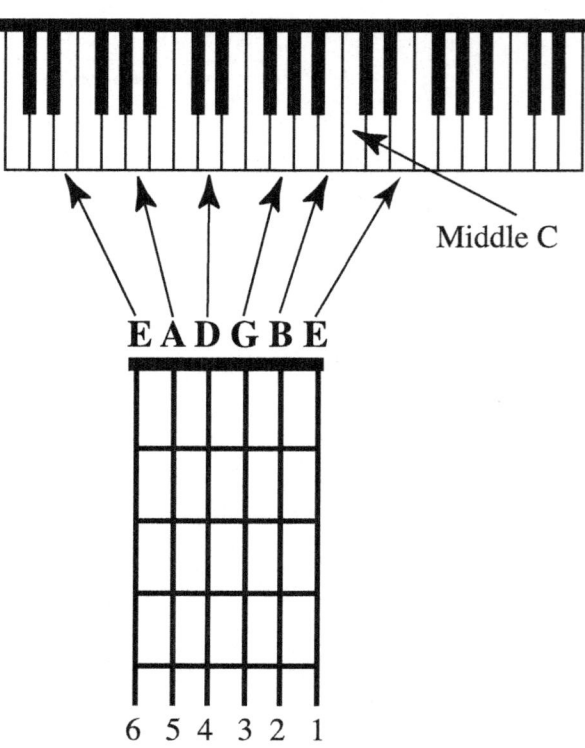

**Note**: If your piano hasn't been tuned recently, the guitar may not agree perfectly with a pitch pipe or tuning fork. Some older pianos are tuned a half step below standard pitch. In this case, use one of the following methods to tune.

## AUDIO TRACKS

You should tune your guitar to the Audio Tracks that accompanies this book so that you will be in tune when you play along with the songs and exercises.

## ELECTRONIC TUNER

An electronic tuner is the fastest and most accurate way to tune a guitar. I highly recommend getting one. They are available for $20 - $50.

# SECTION 2
# THE SONGS

All of the songs in this course are played at two speeds on the Audio Tracks. They are available at the following address on the internet:

http://cvls.com/extras/flatpicking/

# WILL THE CIRCLE BE UNBROKEN

Key of C · Traditional

The first 3 songs are examples of Carter style playing, hitting the melody with the bass notes and strumming.

# WILDWOOD FLOWER

**Key of G**                                                                                                   **Traditional**

9

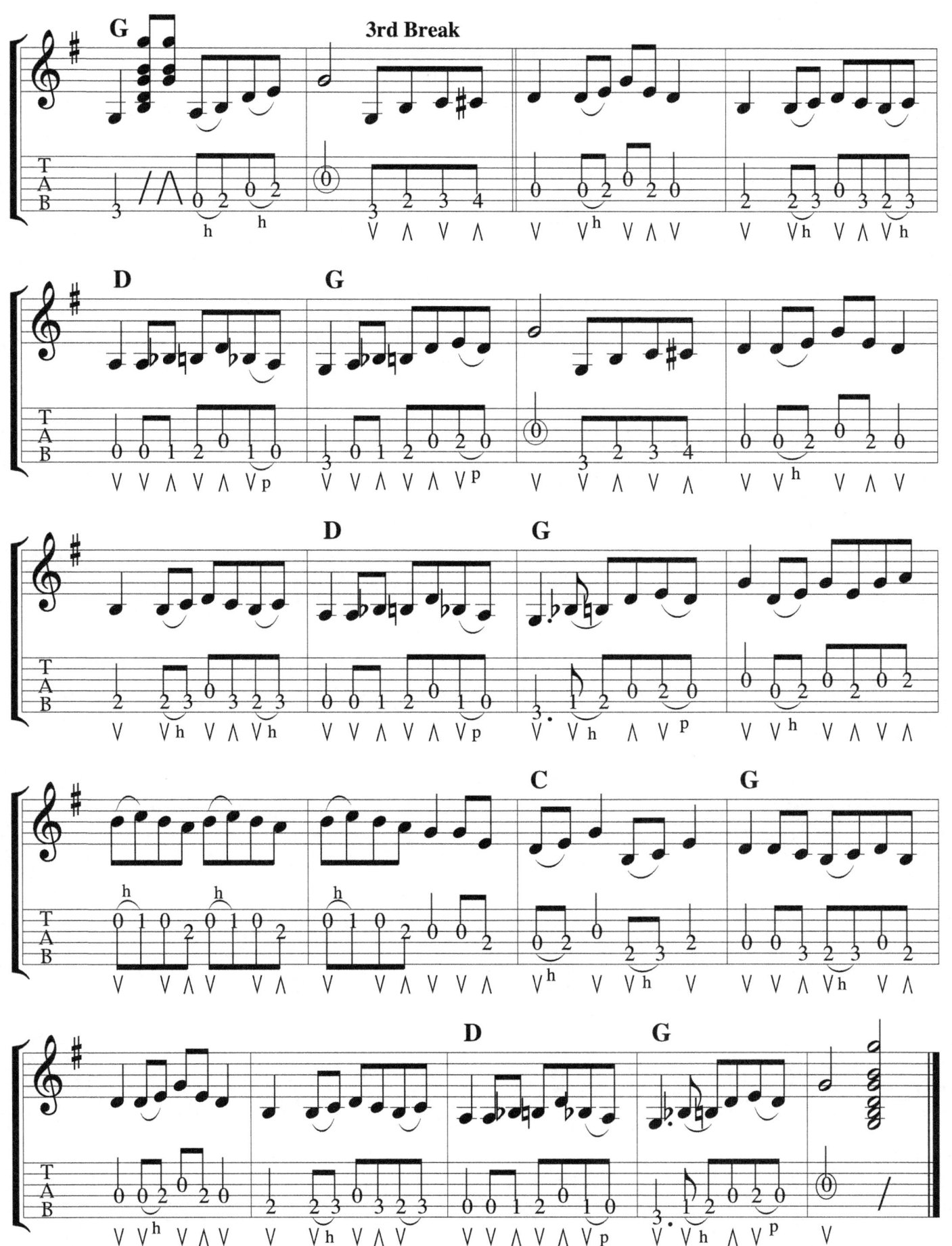

# HOME SWEET HOME

**Key of C**　　　　　　　　　　　　　　　　　　　　　　　　　　　　　　　　　　　　*Traditional*

12

This is an old tune by Stephen Foster made popular in bluegrass circles by Earl Scruggs on the banjo.

In the remaining songs, there will be at least 2 solos or breaks per song. The first break will be a melody break and the 2nd or 3rd break will be "hot licks" and up the neck solos. Practice and learn the first break to each song before you try any of the follow-up breaks.

# CRIPPLE CREEK

**Key of A**  
**Capo 2nd Fret**

*Traditional*

16

**2nd Break**

This is one of the first tunes every banjo player learns and you should know it on guitar. It was also the "Picking & Grinning" song from Hee-Haw.

The lyrics can be found in the *Bluegrass Fakebook*.

# RED HAIRED BOY

**Key of A**  
**Capo 2nd Fret**

Traditional

18

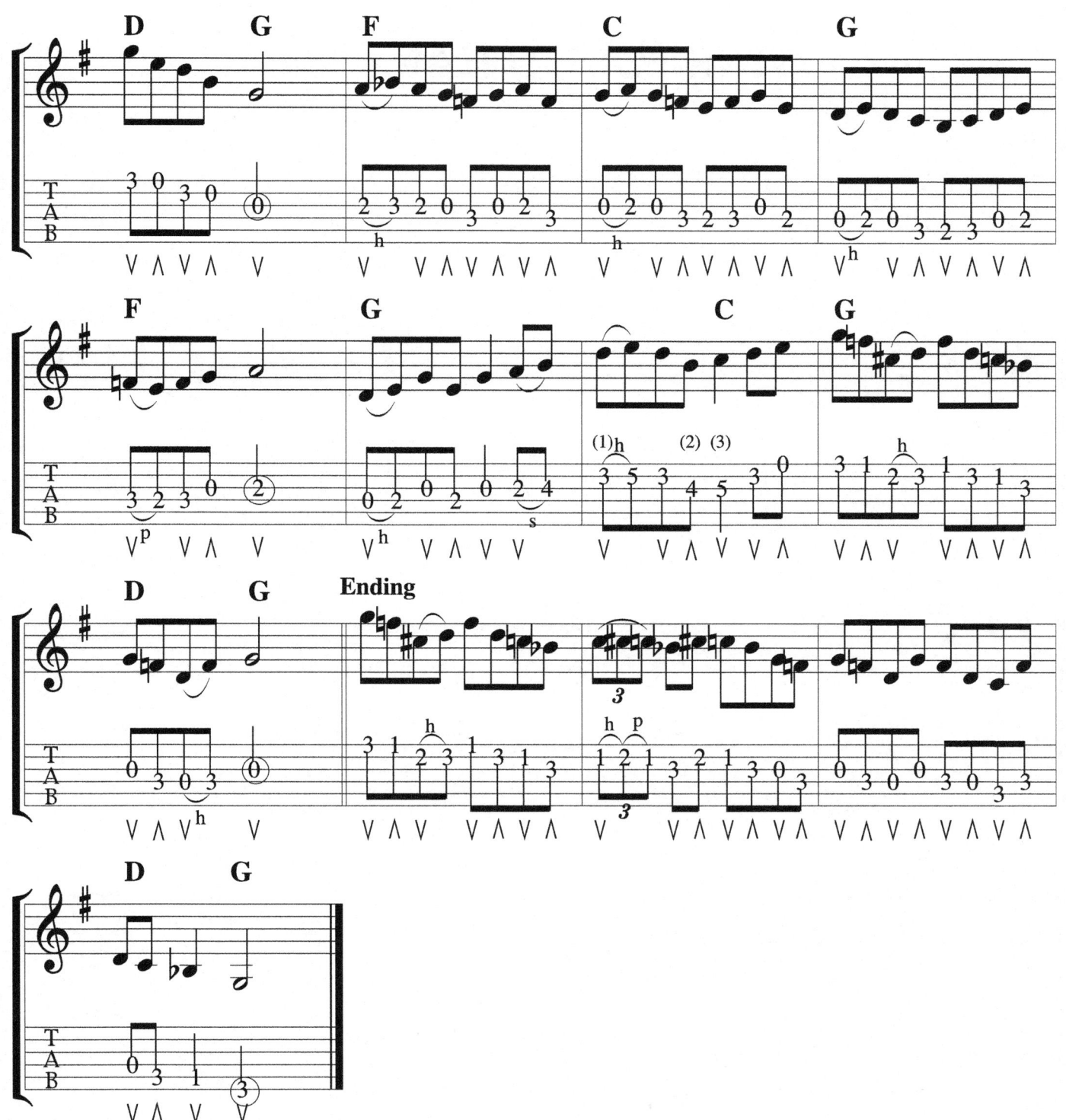

This is an old fiddle tune that is one of my favorites. It's a must for every guitar player.

# NINE POUND HAMMER

**Key of A**
**Capo 2nd Fret**

Traditional

22

This song is a "showcase" tune where we try to show all of the possibilities for composing solos for bluegrass guitar. This arrangement was featured in *Flatpicking Guitar Magazine*. Be sure to listen to the Audio Tracks because there's a lot of syncopation in these breaks.

You can find the rhythm guitar part in *Acoustic Guitar Primer* and the lyrics in the *Bluegrass Fakebook*.

# SALLY GOODIN

**Key of A**
**Capo 2nd Fret**

**Traditional**

This is a standard fiddle tune that's a great jamming song because there are very few chord changes. Just about anything will work here as long as you stay in the key of G.

# OLD JOE CLARK

**Key of A**  
**Capo 2nd Fret**

Traditional

29

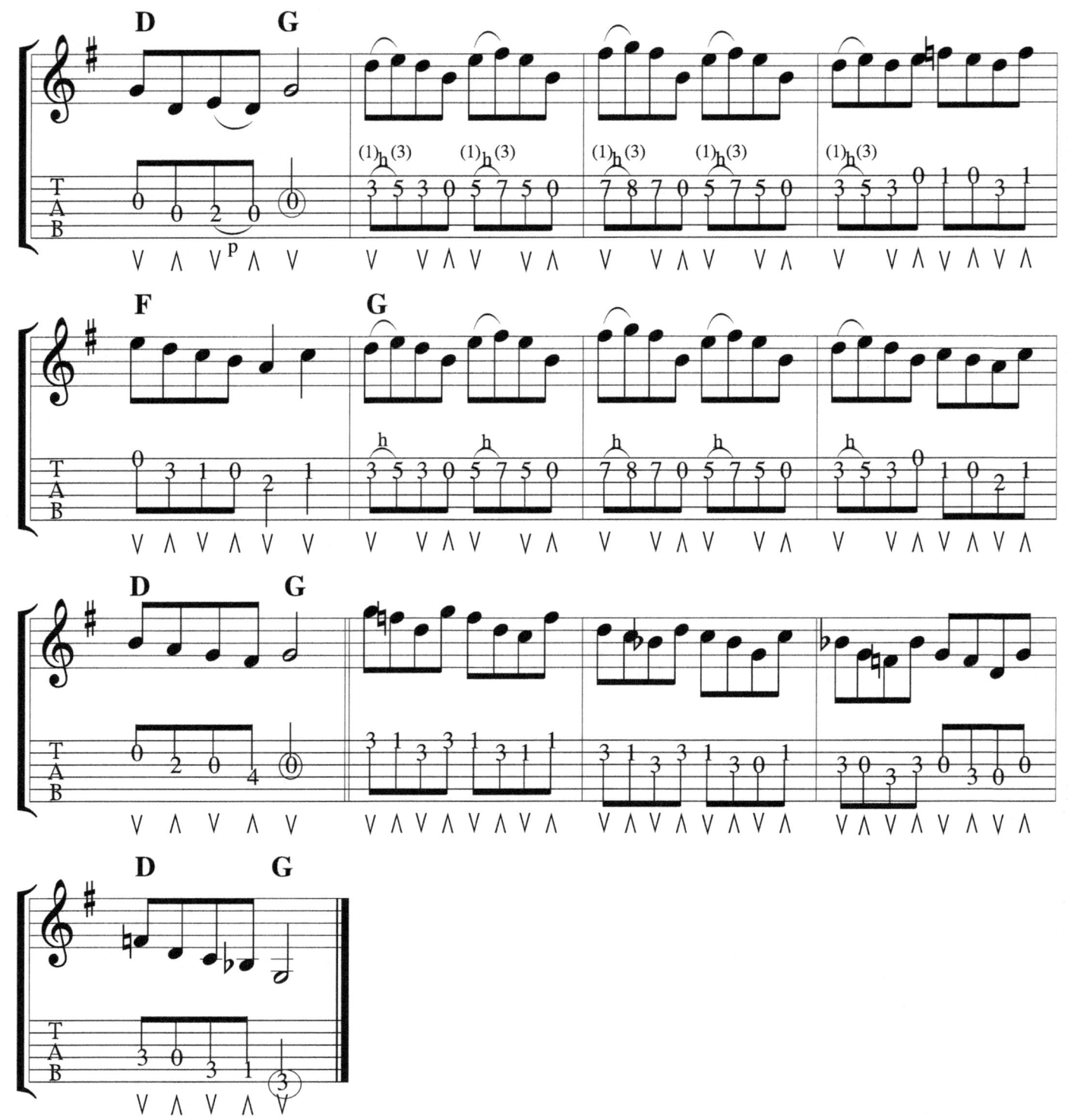

This is another fiddle tune that every bluegrass picker knows. The lyrics are in the *Bluegrass Fakebook*.

# BLACK MOUNTAIN RAG

**Key of A**  
**Capo 2nd Fret**

Traditional

This is a flatpicking guitar standard made popular by Doc Watson. It is also commonly played in the key of C.

# SALT RIVER

**Key of A**  
**Capo 2nd Fret**

**Traditional**

# BILLY IN THE LOWGROUND

**Key of C**                                                                                   **Traditional**

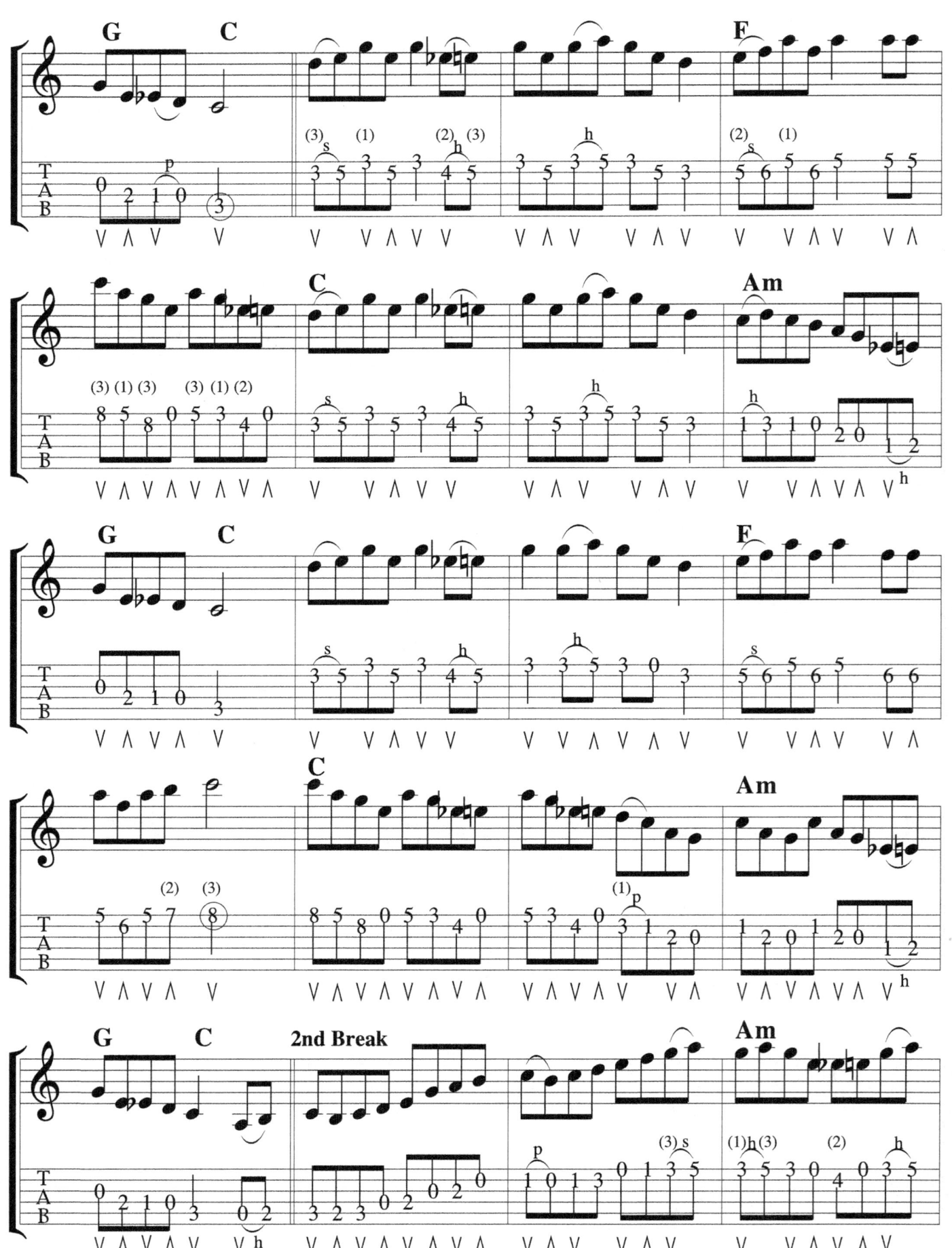

One of my favorite fiddle tunes on the guitar.

# JOHN HARDY

**Key of A**  
**Capo 2nd Fret**

Traditional

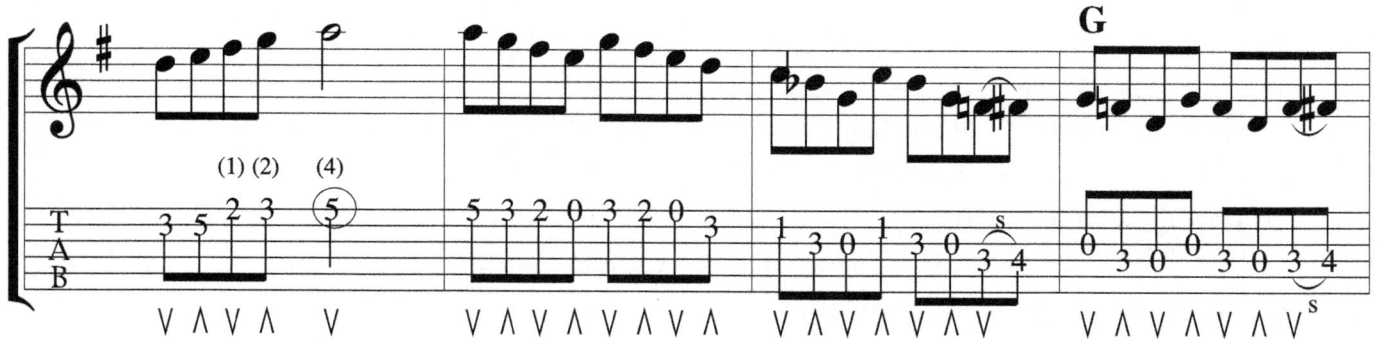
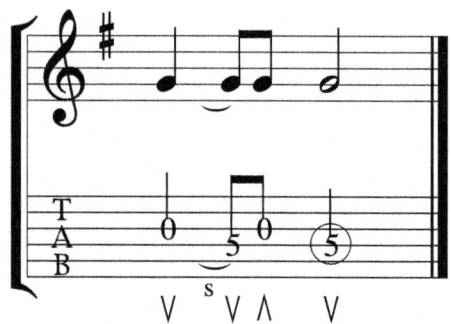

This is another standard that all guitar players should know. A Carter style break is in the *Acoustic Guitar Primer* and the lyrics are in the *Bluegrass Fakebook*.

# CHORD CHART

There is a chord chart on the following page that shows all of the common chords you will encounter. Notice that they are laid out in sequence with all of the different type chords on the same line. For instance, all of the different G chords are on the first line. They are also aligned vertically in finger patterns. For example, all of the 7th chords are in the third column.

The small x on top of the chord diagram means don't strum this string because it would be a note that is not in the chord.

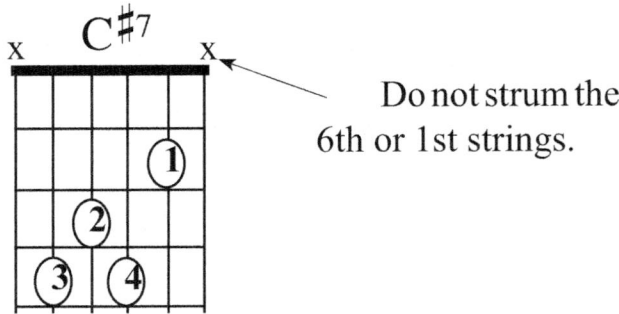

Do not strum the 6th or 1st strings.

The number at the right side of the chord shows the fret position when the chord is moved up the neck..

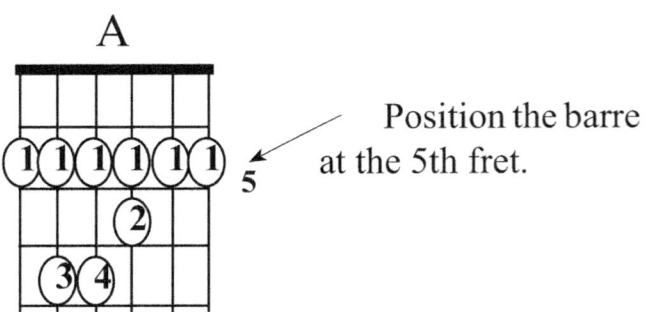

Position the barre at the 5th fret.

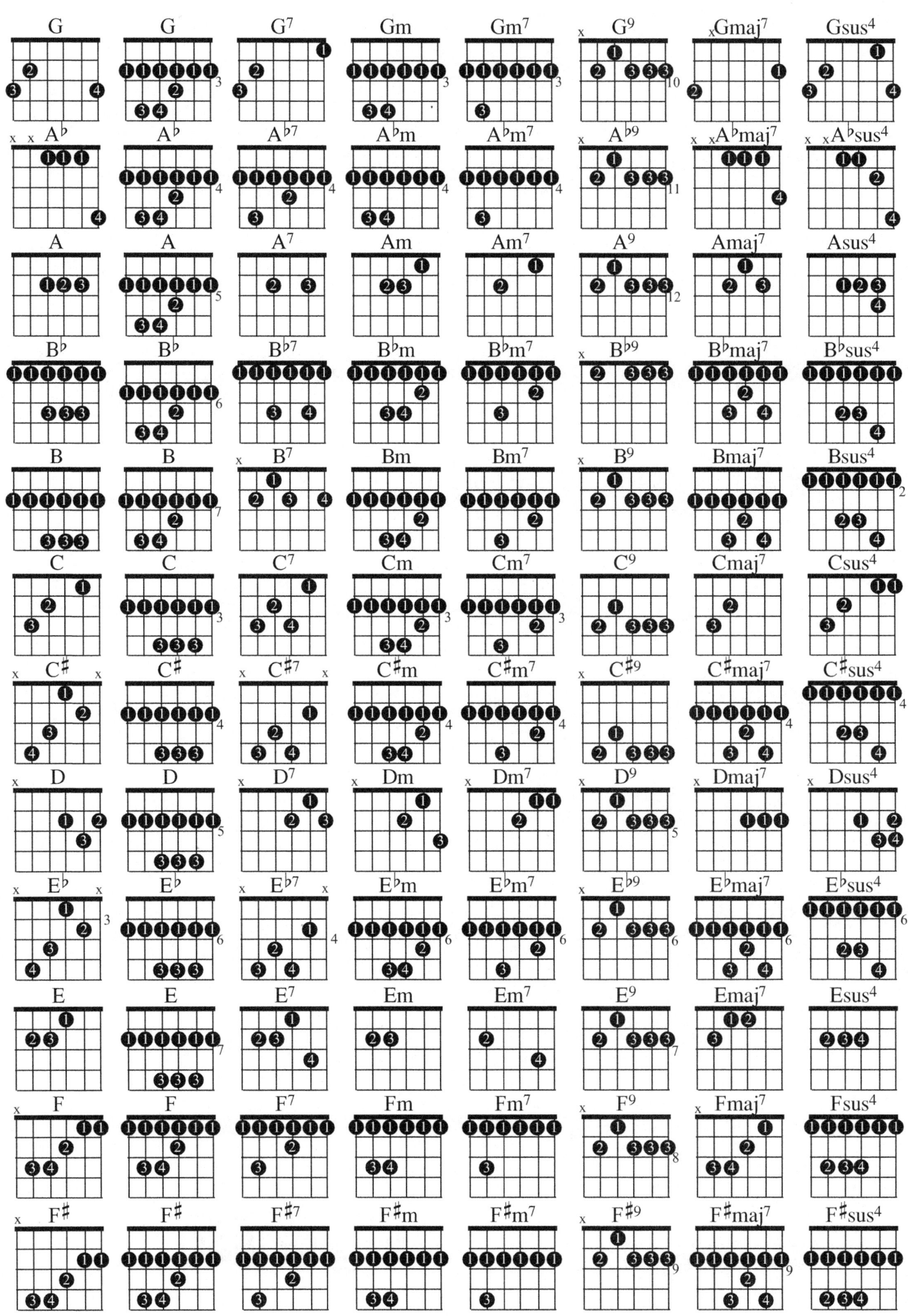

Printed in Great Britain
by Amazon